New England

This book was devised and produced by
Multimedia Publications (UK) Ltd

Editor: Marilyn Inglis
Production: Arnon Orbach
Design: John Strange and Associates
Picture Research: Virginia Landry, Tessa Paul

ISBN 0 8317 6319 1

First published in the United States of
America 1985 by Gallery Books, an imprint of
W. H. Smith Publishers Inc., 112 Madison
Avenue, New York, NY 10016

Typeset by Flowery Typesetters Ltd.
Originated by Imago
Printed in Italy by Sagdos, Milan

New England

C F Perkins

GALLERY BOOKS
An Imprint of W. H. Smith Publishers Inc.
112 Madison Avenue
New York City 10016

CONTENTS

CHAPTER 1

New England Roots

Let's begin with a story. A New England story.

It's about a New Yorker who stops his Cadillac at a rural crossroads in southern New Hampshire. He is miles from anywhere. There are no signposts, no direction markers. Nearby, a farmer is plowing his field.

"Hey, farmer!" shouts the New Yorker impatiently. "Which way is it to New Boston?"

The farmer pulls up his horse, settles the plow in its furrow, thinks about it for a moment. "Dunno," he says at last.

"Which way is Milford, then?"

The farmer scratches his head. "Dunno."

"How about South Weare? Bedford? Goffstown?"

Each question is met with a polite disclaimer. The farmer hasn't heard of *any* of these places. Exasperated, the New Yorker says at last, "Well, you don't know much, do you? You lived around here all your life?"

The farmer considers this for a moment. "Nope," he says carefully. "Not yet."

Perhaps as much as anything else this story captures the special flavor and spirit of New England. The dry wit, the taciturnity, the reticence in speech and manner, the mild distrust of outsiders, but above all the New Englander's feel for place — his sense of permanence and established roots. One lives here in this town because ... because *this* is where one's family lives. One follows this occupation or farms this land because ... well, because one's father had done the same. And *his* father before him.

New Englanders are the ones who stayed, the young men who generations ago did not "go West", the ones who chose instead to squeeze their livelihoods out of the stony soil and harsh climate of New England. New Englanders have a deep feeling for their inhospitable land. Roots grown in such stubborn soil are roots which pierce deep and cling hard.

Nowhere else in America does the past seem so much a part of the living present as in New England. The past is everywhere: in captured cannon still guarding peaceful parks against the return of the Redcoats; in centuries-old historic buildings and lovingly restored colonial villages; in streets which trace former cowpaths; in church ceilings built like inverted boat hulls; in the pragmatic, no-nonsense architecture of private homes; in the layout of tidy villages clustered around church and green; in patterns of settlement which even now echo the days when rivers were the only highways into the interior; but most of all New England's past lives in the character, traditions, and values of its people.

It is easy enough to say that New England values are Puritan values, and certainly there is a degree of truth in this. New England *was* founded by Puritans; serious, high-minded men and women who left everything they had behind in their search for religious freedom. (Religious freedom for themselves that is; they were considerably less scrupulous about religious freedom for others.) And even today there remains a dour, uncompromising way of looking at the world which is as much Puritan as it is New England. But if New England values are Puritan values, they are Puritan values tested and tempered by time, amended and added to by the experiences of fourteen generations in the New World. The harsh realities of the Colonial frontier allowed no room for illusions. The wilderness did not suffer fools. Nor fanatics. Nor the weak and dependent.

Above Plimouth (the old spelling of Plymouth) Plantations, MA. Replica of a Pilgrim house. Note the thatched roof, reminiscent of the Pilgrims' English heritage, and the frame construction. Wood was abundant but every board had to be sawed by hand and hammered into place with wooden pegs.

Right Munroe Tavern, Lexington, MA. A seventeenth-century building used as a gathering place by the Colonists.

Facing page above "If they mean war, let it begin here." The Minuteman Statue, Lexington, MA. Armed with smoothbore musket and powderhorn, the opening battle of the American Revolution was fought here, by men like these.

Facing page below Hancock Clark House, Lexington, MA. John Hancock and Samuel Adams were hiding in this house when Paul Revere rode into Lexington to warn of the approach of the British.

Below The Old State House, Boston MA. From here the British ruled Colonial Massachusetts; from here they proclaimed the hated taxes and acts which were to lose them their New World colonies. This end of the Old State House bears the American Eagle.

The early settlers' choice was simple –
adapt or perish. And adapt they did,
generation after generation, until finally at
some point of transition too subtle for
history to record, Puritan values (much
changed and subdued) became Yankee
values.

Self-reliance, self-restraint, industry,
independence, ingenuity, individualism,
practicality, thrift – Puritan values, yes. But
the Puritan values that helped one survive
on the frontier. And don't ever think that the
New England frontier wasn't a crash course
in survival. Disease, starvation, isolation,
the unforgiving winter, the unyielding soil –
the first New Englanders clung to the thin
edge of existence, and each generation that
followed seemed to face new tribulations.

Right John Harvard, Cambridge graduate,
Puritan minister, and philanthropist. He left his
library and almost a thousand pounds – half his
estate – to the small, struggling college in
Cambridge, MA, which was later to bear his
name. Harvard's endowment today is over
$1 billion. Founded in 1636 (and re-named in
1639) Harvard is the oldest institution of
higher learning in the United States.

Facing page The State Capital, Providence, RI.
After St Peter's in Rome, this is the second
largest unsupported marble dome in the world.

Below "As they honor their dead, so shall you
know them". The stern beauty of this Vermont
cemetery speaks of the values by which these
New Englanders once lived.

No sooner had nature been sufficiently tamed to assure the Colonists' continued survival in the New World, than there were flare-ups with the Indians – raids, scalpings, kidnappings. And no sooner had the Indians been subdued than the early settlers found themselves confronted by the enemy within – the dark underside of the human spirit which was to emerge in the Salem witch trials but which ran through all the Colonies. And then New Englanders found themselves in the bloody forefront of the Revolution. The brief prosperity after the Revolution was followed by the collapse of the whaling and shipping industries in the nineteenth century and the collapse of the textile industry in the twentieth. For three hundred years New Englanders have lived with danger and hardship. Such a history leaves its mark on the people.

"Save," says the New Englander. "Mend. Patch up. Make do." "Waste not, want not." "A place for everything – everything in its place," or as Robert Frost puts the same thought slightly differently, "Good fences make good neighbors."

One does not have to listen hard to hear in the folk wisdom of New England the echoes of a people left to their own resources on the brittle edge of a new continent, separated by 3000 miles of hostile ocean from any hope of help. But gradually the wilderness was tamed and just as gradually, over the next two hundred years, other kinds of Englishmen arrived in the Colonies. So did peoples of other ethnic backgrounds – Germans and Scots, and Scotch-Irish – people with different values and different views on life. All of a sudden the Puritans were no longer the dominant group in New England society; the time came when they were no longer the majority. A new country had grown up around them. Their direct influence waned and ultimately disappeared but they left behind a spiritual and intellectual tradition which is part and parcel of the New England heritage.

Consider for instance the old Yankee grandmother who died not too long ago in upstate Vermont. The good lady had outlived all her kin and had died intestate, so it was decided to auction off her worldly goods for the benefit of the local church.

As the grandmother's effects were auctioned, it became obvious that even by New England standards she was a model of those Yankee virtues of thrift, industry, and order – a saint who had never thrown away a thing in her life. One of the last items auctioned was a half-filled jar labeled "Bits of String too Short to Use." Only out-of-

staters thought it odd when this item came under the hammer. Native New Englanders hardly batted an eyelid. They understood. They approved. In fact it was a Vermonter who bought the jar! After all, the price was right and one never knew when bits of string like that might come in handy. Or a jar.

Long before the Puritans arrived, of course, New England was inhabited by Indians – descendants of the hunters who crossed the great land bridge from Asia in Stone Age times, say about 20 000 years ago. The New England Indians were members of the eastern branch of the Algonkians, a hunting/fishing/farming people, mainly peaceful, who lived on the coast and inland along the important rivers, Mohicans, Nipmucs, Wampanoags, Pequawkets, Picscataquas, we hardly remember the names of those once proud and powerful tribes. Maine celebrates a state Indian Day, Rhode Island holds an annual Narraganset Indian pow-wow, but other than that few traces of the eastern woods Indians remain beyond exhibits in museums and romanticized pictures in books. They are now ghosts in their own land who survive as little more than place names. Only in the words they have bequeathed to the language such as "canoe", "toboggan", "skunk", do we catch a glimpse of their vanished culture. Only in the magic of their place names do we recall that Indians lived here and once loved this land too. Massachusetts – "place of the great hill"; Connecticut – "on the tidal river"; Pawtucket – "falls at the mouth of the river"; Uncanoonuc Mountains – "hills like woman's breasts".

The first Europeans to come in contact with these Indians were probably the Vikings who may have established colonies on the New England coast as early as the eleventh century. It's not clear how long the Vikings stayed, but for whatever reason,

Facing page A young Vermonter helps with the annual harvest of sap from the maple trees. The sap will be boiled down into maple sugar and maple syrup – about 40 gallons of sap for one gallon of syrup. Vermont is America's leading producer of maple syrup.

Above and below The sapping season takes place in spring but the woods are still deep in snow and a horse-drawn sleigh is often the most efficient way to haul heavy loads to the saphouse. To make maple sugar: bore a hole in maple trees in the springtime; collect gallons of the colorless, tasteless sap; then boil it for several days over a roaring fire. The Colonists learned this trick from the Indians.

their colonies failed and the Indians were left peacefully to themselves for another four hundred years. In the century following Columbus's great discovery, the New England coast was visited by a variety of French and English explorers – Verrazano, Cartier, Cabot, Gosnold, Gilbert – but there was little contact with the Indians.

When at last the Puritans arrived – starving, friendless palefaces, woefully ignorant of their new environment – the New England Indians were compassionate enough, and short-sighted enough, to feed them and help them to survive that first winter. The Indians taught the Colonists how to hunt and fish, how to farm and plant. They even took part in the Pilgrims' first Thanksgiving. For their pains the Indians were slaughtered, infected with white man's diseases, deprived of their land, and driven westward – a pattern that was to repeat itself time and again. All too soon the further history of New England became the history of the Puritans.

And what do we know of the Puritans? Well, we know that they landed on Plymouth Rock in 1620 and founded the first permanent colony in North America. Right? Sorry – wrong. As it happens, the English were rather late arrivals in the New World. By the time the Pilgrims stepped ashore that freezing December day the French had already built a flourishing town called Quebec; the Dutch had settled in numbers

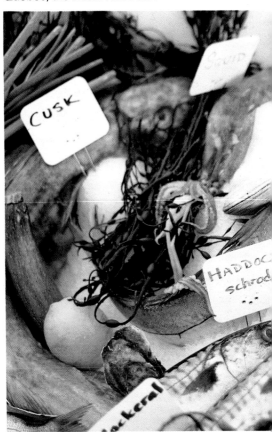

near Albany, New York; and the Spanish administered a vast New World empire which even at that early date contained almost two hundred cities and villages, and a *Spanish* population alone of nearly 200 000. The Pilgrims were not even the first English settlement in the New World – Jamestown (VA) had been founded more than a decade earlier. In fact, the Puritans weren't even the first English colony in New England – an unsuccessful colony had been founded on the Maine coast in 1607.

Puritan history became important because it is the history of the winners, the settlers who won the race for that part of the New World we now call the United States. By the middle of the seventeenth century the Puritans and their descendants and allies had driven out the Dutch; by the end of the eighteenth they had decimated the Indians, pushed aside the French, and even usurped the British; before the end of the second decade of the nineteenth century, they had deposed the Spanish.

It is important too in understanding their history to remember that the Pilgrim Fathers were Englishmen. This is why we speak the language we speak, and have the sort of laws and the form of government that we have. The rights and freedoms that we cherish are the traditional rights of Englishmen, rights which Puritans brought with them – habeus corpus, trial by jury, government by consent of the governed,

no taxation without representation. It was after all only when the mother country tried to deny these fundamental English rights to Englishmen born in the Colonies that the Revolution began.

Had a different nation won this early colonial scramble, the subsequent history of our country would be very different, and so would our view of the Puritans. If the Dutch, for example, had won, history would have spoken of the Puritans, if at all, as rather quirky interlopers who settled briefly in the region north of New Amsterdam before being moved on.

But the Dutch didn't win.

And the rest is history.

Let's end this chapter with another New England story.

The flinty independence of New Englanders is, of course, legendary – as is their dislike of Federal authority all those miles away in Washington. Pity the poor New Englander then who struggled for hours filling in one of those endless Government forms. When at last he came to the end, he noticed a neat little box marked DO NOT WRITE IN THIS SPACE. FOR OFFICIAL USE ONLY. Perhaps this New Englander spoke for us all when he boldly scrawled a typically New England message in the little box.

"I shall write," he wrote, "where I goddam please."

Facing page left Weather-beaten clapboard, a pebbled beach and ruined lobster trap make this New England shore scene a study in textures.

Bottom Lobster buoys. Each color pattern is registered and as individual as a cattleman's brand.

Center Some of the rich harvest of New England waters on display at a Seafest on Nantucket Island.

Below Basketweaving. Reviving the old crafts at Sturbridge Village, MA, an accurate reconstruction of a New England town in the early 1800s. Well worth a visit.

CHAPTER 2

Forests, Mountains and Water

New England is a feast for the eyes – a scenic spectacular of mountain and field, coast and forest, filtered through an ever-changing kaleidoscope of four very distinct and very different seasons. Adding to this natural beauty is the presence of man himself. New England is one of those rare places where, like the Swiss Alps, the works of man, intentionally or not, seem to enhance the natural landscape. Here the presence of man does not intrude. Modern New England has its urban sprawl, of course, but much more characteristically it has quiet villages clustered around central squares, white steepled churches and bustling little harbors, stone walls greened over with moss and red barns stark against the snow, covered bridges and winding roads. In New England man's works add a quiet charm to the beauty of the natural scene.

Of the natural landscape, the most spectacular element is the mountains. New England is mountain country, the northernmost outpost of the mighty Appalachians that stretch from Georgia all the way to lonely Mount Katahdin in Maine (the first part of the United States to receive the sun of each new day). The Appalachians are at their highest and most spectacular in the White Mountains of Maine and New Hampshire where the naked peaks of the Presidential Range jut well above the timberline. Tallest is Mount Washington (6288 feet), which is also one of the two tallest peaks east of the Mississippi. Between Mount Washington and the Arctic wastes thousands of miles to the north stands little except miles and miles of empty tundra. The prevailing Northwesterlies have an uninterrupted sweep of thousands of miles. Not surprisingly, the climate above the timberline is virtually sub-arctic with plant and insect life more akin to Hudson's Bay

than to New England. The highest wind velocity ever measured on earth (231 mph) was recorded atop Mount Washington. The speed and viciousness with which the weather can change is surprising even for mountain country. The hiker is advised to be well prepared and knowledgeable. More than one life has been lost by under-estimating these seemingly gentle peaks.

The Green Mountains of Vermont run southward the whole length of the state. They are lower, greener, and more wooded than the White Mountains, altogether more human in scale, and have an understated beauty of their own. South of the Green Mountains are the Taconics and Berkshires of western Massachusetts—spectacular in the fall—the Taconics just reaching into northwestern Connecticut. Rhode Island alone of the New England states has no significant mountain areas, the highest point being Jerimoth Hill (812 feet).

New England is served by an excellent road system that makes the mountains accessible year round. Many of the area's resorts now stay open all year and cater to the summer visitor as much as the winter sportsman. For those wishing to experience the mountains first hand, there is also a network of trails, huts, and shelters maintained by the Appalachian Mountain Club. There are hikes and climbs of every degree of difficulty.

Above Horses will plow where it's too steep for tractors, a handy fact to remember in Vermont, where farms clamber up and down the slopes of the Green Mountains.

Left Peacham, VT. The archetypal New England village. The white steepled church, the cluster of houses, the corbeled barns, all nestling in some of the most glorious and unspoiled countryside in America.

Facing page above Flowering dogwood. Laurel and rhododendrons are other shrubs that flower spectacularly in the spring. Visitors from all over the world come to marvel at the dogwood display on Greenfield Hill, near Fairfield, CT.

Facing page below Aroostook County, ME. The deep fertile soil yields one of the largest potato crops in the US despite a growing season only a hundred days long.

The rugged coastline of New England is a painter's dream. Pine forests plunging down to the sea; rocky ledges enduring the onslaught of the Atlantic; lighthouses and foghorns; offshore islands and tidal marshes. The waters are dotted with the sails of small yachts and windjammers; further offshore one still sees the occasional square rigger, reminders of the time when Yankee clippers ruled the seas.

But picturesque as all this may be, New England is still a working coast, and this is part of its charm. Moored right in with the acres of pleasure craft are trawlers and lobster boats, Coast Guard cutters and sleek gray naval vessels. Ashore there are colorful shacks festooned with lobster buoys, grizzled fishermen mending nets, pierheads stacked high with lobster traps and boxes of fish. Busy shipyards build anything from Grand Banks dories to nuclear submarines.

The most scenic part of the coast is arguably Acadia National Park in Maine, the only National Park east of the Mississippi. Centered on Bar Harbor and Frenchman's Bay, Acadia is a perfect combination of surf, rock, and forest – the coast much as it looked when the Puritans first saw it. Mount

Cadillac, a naked granite peak atop Mount Desert Island in the heart of the Park, is the highest point on the East Coast of the United States – in fact, the highest point on the Atlantic between Labrador and Rio de Janeiro. Further to the south is the haunting loneliness of the Cape Cod National Seashore, with its shifting sand dunes and wheeling sea birds. Further south still are the wind-swept fills of Nantucket Island, perhaps the remotest and wildest part of the coast.

New England is heavily forested, with deciduous hardwoods predominating in the south, and spruce, hemlock, fir, cedar and pine in the north. Maine has many times more pine trees than people (or anything else for that matter). Not for nothing is it known as the Pine Tree State.

Once, the King of Britain owned all the pines in New England and special teams roamed the wilderness cutting the best and tallest trees as masts for His Majesty's Navy. Many a New England town even today has its Mast Road. It is surprising that New England is as heavily forested as it is, for as the early Colonists pushed inland from the seacoast, the first thing they did was to hack down the forest, burn it, and

Facing page above An abandoned farm near Danville, VT. During the nineteenth century, many farms were abandoned as New England turned from being a farming to a manufacturing society.

Facing page below Early morning mists and the rolling slopes of the Green Mountains make a perfect reflection in the West River, near Brattleboro, VT.

Left Black-eyed Susans are strewn prodigally over this Vermont meadow.

Below The steep hillside and magnificent herd of Holsteins are typical of a Vermont hill farm. Holsteins produce more milk than other breeds of cattle.

then try to farm what was left.

As the rural population declined in the nineteenth century, however, farms were abandoned on a large scale and the patient forest reclaimed its own. Hard as it may be to believe when contemplating a hundred-foot white pine, most of the heavy forest cover we know today actually comprises second and third growth trees.

It is the forest cover too which gives us that most characteristically New England scenic spectacular of all – the autumn. Each season in New England has its own admirers but in the final analysis winter, spring and summer in New England aren't that different from winter, spring and summer anywhere. A hot day is a hot day, and snow is snow; they look and feel much the same whether one is in Boston or Boise.

Autumn, however, is quite another matter. Only in New England is there that special combination of vegetation, soil, natural landscape, and climate which produces full-scale autumn extravaganzas. Other falls are pale second-raters compared to New England's. At the height of the fall, it is like being transported to another planet. Whole mountains are ablaze with yellow, gold, scarlet, orange, and purple, shimmering with intensity, a sea of color as far as the eye can reach, dappled here and there by the dark stripes of evergreens.

Visitors from all over the world come to

Above Remains of old schooners, near Wiscasset, ME. Yankee Clippers once ruled these seas – in fact, they still hold the record for the fastest sail crossing of the Atlantic.

Left Harvest time. The first frost of the year glazes this New England pumpkin field.

Facing page below A New England village in the winter. The straight lines of trees mark stone walls and summer fields buried deep in snow. Even in these modern times it is still possible for the remoter villages to be snowbound for days on end. East Corinth, VT.

Facing page above Barre (VT) granite quarry in winter. Quarrying is a year-round business. The Rock of Ages Quarry in Barre is the world's largest.

New England in the fall. Nor are they disappointed. But the casual visitor can never know the full glory of fall any more than a tourist viewing a waterfall can know the full majesty of the river that spawned it. To the New Englander, autumn is not just a few spectacular days near the end of October; it is the whole season from beginning to end, the months-long sweep of time, the anticipation of its coming and the sadness of its going. Autumn is the haze that clings to the hills in the mornings, the smell of burning leaves, the light-sweater days and extra-blanket nights, the golden sun of Indian Summer; it is the signs of harvest – corn shucks and pumpkins, empty fields, cider apples and squash; it is chipmunks scuttling past with cheeks bulging, the sudden disappearance of the robins, the V's and F's of ducks etching the sky.

In the high north, autumn begins as early as late August. The goldenrod loses its color. The most sensitive leaves, blueberry and sumac, begin to "color up" like the first tentative trickles of the springs that feed a river. Daily the bands of color around the edges of the leaves grow toward the center;

Above Dark green evergreens set off the blazing colors of an autumn hillside. The cottage has been locked and shuttered and now waits for the winter that is never far behind.

Right A covered bridge in NH framed by maples in the height of their autumn color. Tne covering was designed to protect the bridges from the ravages of the weather.

Facing page left A farmer loads the last bales of hay into his barn to feed his cattle in winter. New England schoolchildren can taste the difference in the milk when the cows are switched from summer grazing to winter feed (and vice versa).

Facing page above Storm clouds gathering over the Town Hall of Strafford, VT, cannot obscure the magnificence of this autumn day.

daily, like rivulets merging into a stream, other trees succumb to "the turn". A bush here, a small tree there. First birch, alder, beech and poplar, then more stubborn trees like maple and oak, and finally, most stubborn of all, the needles of deciduous softwoods like larch and tamarack. One day it is still summer, green everywhere; the next it is autumn. By late September autumn is a strong young river; by late October it is a torrent.

Beautiful, yes. But melancholy too. No person who loves fall watches it without sadness. Soon all this beauty will be gone. And there is no holding it back. Like a river plunging headlong into the sea, October turns into November. The colors of autumn fade to dun, the leaves wither and fall. Bare branches begin to poke through, then to predominate. One night there is a high wind and the next, it seems, the branches are bare. The first frost coats the leaves where they lie. The skies grow leaden, the mornings more chill. There is a hint of snow . . .

Previous page High tide, Stonington, ME. The Maine coast has a high tidefall. Platforms on stilts are used to bypass mudflats of low tide.

Above Lobster pots, Bar Harbor, ME. The trap in the middle of the second row gives us a lobster's eye view of the process. Lobsters crawl through this hole seeking bits of fish left by the fishermen and then can't get out again. It's that simple. The traps must, by law, be emptied every day, otherwise cannibalistic lobsters will devour each other.

Left A lobster shack on the Maine coast. Such shacks are used mainly for storage and do not require subtleties like windows. Wooden shingles are an inexpensive way of weatherproofing buildings in timber-rich New England.

Facing page center Pemaquid Light contemplates its own reflection in a tidal pool. The rock strata have been turned on edge by the mighty earth convulsions which thrust up this coast millions of years ago.

Facing page left Plymouth, MA. A shrewd Yankee shopkeeper knows how to catch the tourists' eye with this display of lobster buoys and lifebuoys, hawsers and oars, lobster pots and nets.

Facing page above Newport Bridge, RI. This magnificent bridge guards the entrance to Narraganset Bay. The hump in the middle ensures that large ocean-going ships have access to Providence, Pawtucket, Warwick and other Rhode Island ports.

Facing page below Sea, surf, sky, naked rock, and pine – the quintessential coast of Maine.

Left Storm fences slow down the movement of the dunes, an important priority at Dionis Beach on Nantucket Island. Similar storm fences are used in winter to slow down drifting snow.

Below Seal Harbor, ME. Part of Acadia National Park. Vice-president Nelson Rockefeller once had a summer home near here. Vice-president George Bush's home is just down the coast in Kennebunkport.

Outdoor Pleasures

New England is a sportsman's paradise. It is a rare sport indeed which is not enjoyed in one form or another in New England, but the region is most famous for its winter sports. Skiing, skating, sledding, snowshoeing, snowmobiling, skijoring, the list seems endless, traditional sports mixing with modern ones.

Every state in New England has its own ski areas but the further north one goes, of course, the taller the mountains and the deeper the snow. It is possible to ski as early as November and (for fantatics willing to make the climb to Tuckerman's Ravine) as late as June. Many would argue that the best skiing of all comes in March and April, when the sun shines and the snow "corns up." Skiing in shirtsleeves and shorts is a common sight in springtime New England, but it can make a sliding fall a rather unpleasant experience!

Each resort has its own special flavor and feel but Stowe (VA) is typical of the larger New England resorts. Here, two mountains are served by a variety of chairlifts, T-bars, and rope tows; runs are graded from nursery slopes to trails like the Nosedive which challenge Olympians – all are regularly patrolled; accommodation is abundant and priced for every pocketbook; the roads are well plowed; and the town of Stowe itself is filled with a variety of interesting shops and après-ski activity.

For purists who scorn uphill lifts and other such frivolities, cross-country skiing has become increasingly popular and there are now whole resorts set aside exclusively for ski touring. The ultimate purist's challenge, however, is Tuckerman's Ravine, a vast snowbowl high on Mount Washington (NH). The sides of the Ravine are too steep in themselves to hold snow, but over the course of the winter the Ravine fills up with snow blown off the top of Mount Washington. Avalanches and icefalls

and abominable weather make the Ravine too dangerous to ski in the winter, but in the spring the snow settles and the skiing is superb. The only way to get to the Ravine is by a back-breaking two-hour climb from the valley floor, so skiing at Tuckerman's tends to be an experience for the dedicated. The headwall is so steep that one does not fall *down* so much as *off*, and a fall at Tuckerman's is not for the faint of heart. Despite this, the run down the summit cone of Mount Washington followed by, if you dare, the plunge over the Tuckerman headwall is one of the supreme challenges and experiences in American skiing.

For those interested in less energetic forms of skiing there are frequent jumping competitions all over New England, where in relative comfort the spectator can watch top jumpers from all over the world. The largest hill in New England is the 260-foot monster at Berlin (NH) – a jump so large that one is no longer jumping so much as flying. The longest jumps on the big hill stretch the length of a football field!

If snow is part of the New England winter, then so is ice – and the frozen ponds, lakes and rinks of the region offer a variety of activity. Almost every town and city has a pond that it keeps clear of snow for skaters – and a spectacular sight it is. Parkas and colorful hats, scarves and mittens, snakes of children playing crack-the-whip, toddlers on double-bladed runners, oldsters skating gingerly around the outside. In one corner will be serious figure skaters, in another, gangs of boys playing hockey. Often there is an open-air fire in a nearby metal barrel and

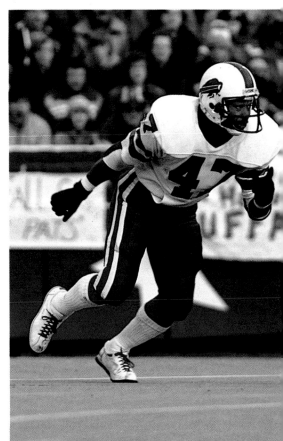

all ages come and sit and talk while they thaw out frozen noses and toes.

Hockey is a widespread schoolboy sport in New England, though increasingly it tends to be played indoors and in organized leagues. Serious amateur hockey leagues and semi-professional leagues flourish, and the standard of play is very high indeed, well worth a visit if you have never seen hockey played. The Boston Bruins are New England's only fully professional ice hockey team.

The long sweep of the prevailing winds keeps the larger lakes clear of snow, much to the delight of the iceboaters. Iceboats

Facing page left Boston Celtics ruled professional basketball for more than ten years in the 1950s and 1960s, a dynasty unequalled by other New England teams.

Center Pro football is part of the sports scene in New England.

Left The Boston Bruins' goal keeper is armored like a medieval knight. In the rough and tumble of the National Hockey League, he has to be!

Above Marcus Halevi signs autographs for eager youngsters. Fenway Park, home of the Red Sox, is the most eccentrically shaped and (with Wrigley Field, Chicago) one of the most charming ball parks in the major leagues.

look like sailboats mounted on skates and work much the same way, although few sailboats are capable of the 70 to 80 miles per hour thrills of the iceboats! On some New England lakes, the ice freezes so thick that they hold stock car racing on it. Even with chains and specially adapted cars the action is fast and dangerous.

Most towns have a special hill that they block off to traffic during winter so that local children can use it for sledding and tobogganing. The traditional bobsled is disappearing but it is still possible to see ten-man bobs laden with laughing children and adults careening spectacularly downhill. In smaller towns it is not unusual to see local sportsmen out skijoring after a snowfall, being towed along behind cars. In some resorts, it is still possible to enjoy skijoring in the old-fashioned way – behind a galloping horse.

In northern New England, the French-Canadian population has taken up snowshoeing in a large way, forming themselves into snowshoe clubs which pursue every form of snowshoeing from trekking into the wilderness to racing for trophies. Annual world championships are attended by snowshoers from all over New England and Quebec. When they gather in their colorful uniforms, parading down the main streets of towns, snowshoes slung on their backs, they make a decorative and spectacular sight – but not all their conviviality can be attributed to *high* spirits alone, and it is a prudent citizen who keeps a low profile when *les raquetteurs* are in town.

Technology has overtaken traditional New England winter pastimes, mainly in the form of snowmobiling. Snowmobiles have made accessible parts of New England which in the past were snowbound for several months of the year. The snowmobile's smelly and noisy presence is not to everyone's taste, however, and regulations now set out exactly when and where snowmobiles may be used.

Although winter sports hold sway from Thanksgiving to Easter there is no slacking of sporting activity during other months of the year. Hunting is an important autumn sport, drawing hunters from all over the eastern seaboard. White-tailed deer are the main quarry but in the northern states it is also possible to hunt bear and moose. Most states now have a short bow and arrow season for deer before the regular season opens. Duck, pheasant, partridge, rabbit, lynx and bobcat are some of the other game hunted in New England. The accessibility of the hunting areas to modern transport has meant a lot of inexperienced

Above Reliable snowfall, carefully graded slopes, and regularly patrolled trails reward these skiers at Killington, VT. The same high standards are found in other New England resorts.

Right Dog sledding, Mirror Lake. Dog sled racing is a popular winter spectacle in New England, for spectator and participant alike.

city hunters roaming the woods with high-powered rifles. There was a time when the New England outback was a dangerous place in the autumn – for farm animals as well as humans. One farmer took to painting "COW" on his livestock (it didn't do him much good as it turned out). The notorious "sound shot" (if you hear something, shoot) was perhaps the most pernicious offender. A well-conducted campaign of education has improved the habits and skills of hunters in recent years, but careless and amoral people still do go into the woods and, sad to say, it is a rare season which is not marred by at least one needless hunting tragedy.

The great hurricane of 1938 blew down the fences of an animal reserve in New Hampshire and some of the exhibits escaped into the wild, including some European black boar. Not surprisingly, the boar flourished in a climate and temperate woodland much like their native environment and, although they are rare, New Hampshire may be the only place outside Europe where it is possible to shoot wild European boar. As a result of the same hurricane, by the way, an elephant also escaped and was for a while roaming the New Hampshire countryside. It has been alleged that some of the local hunters had to be forcibly restrained from hauling out their heavy artillery and trying to bag him. There was nothing in New Hampshire's strict game laws which *prohibited* elephant hunting, after all. There wasn't even a closed season. So why not? Eventually the elephant was safely returned to his pen, but there are some who still assert that New Hampshire is the only state where you could once enjoy elephant hunting!

If New England hunting is good, its fishing is spectacular. The dedicated fisherman can find year-round fishing, both fresh and salt water, for every age and degree of skill. New England waters have been well fished but not over-fished, and most state fish and game authorities are careful to keep lakes and streams well stocked – and well regulated.

Opening day of the trout season will see some of the most popular spots lined with fishermen, rods poised in the pre-dawn darkness, waiting for the first glimmer of the sun when fishing may begin. Some local authorities set aside specially stocked ponds for children. Few children who fish these ponds on opening day return empty-handed and the look on their faces is enough to make sure that the adults don't go home empty-handed either.

As well as trout (brook, brown, lake and rainbow) one may also fish for salmon –

Above Snowmobiling has taken off in a large way in New England – so much so that the deep woods are criss-crossed with trails reserved for their use. Special associations now regulate their use.

Left World sled dog championships are held every year in Laconia, NH. Contestants mush past large crowds of spectators.

Right The Berkshire Hills, MA. Hot air ballooning is a new sport in New England.

Below Ocean racing yacht, *Charisma*, jockeys for position at the start of a race off Newport, R.I.

both landlocked and (in Maine) migratory. Most of the states south of Maine have now introduced tough anti-pollution laws in an attempt to lure the Atlantic salmon back to their rivers.

Besides game fish, the ponds and lakes of New England also abound with coarse fish such as small and large mouth bass, pickerel (which fight as hard and taste as good as any game fish), white and yellow perch, and horned pout. New England is also noted for ice fishing, and in the winter lakes are beaded with fishermen's huts sledged out onto the ice for the season. Each hut is surrounded by a necklace of "sets" – flags on spring traps poised over holes drilled in the ice, waiting for unsuspecting fish.

The sea fishing is also superb. From piers and rowboats, from headlands and offshore rocks, it is a poor fisherman indeed who cannot find a rich abundance of mackerel, pollock, flounder, halibut, cunner, hake, cod and haddock. Offshore, the most

Facing page below Canoe racing, Moose River, Rockwood, ME. Canoes are still the most efficient way to get around in the remoter part of the New England wilderness.

Left The winner and new Champ! *Australia II*, flying her spinnaker, takes the lead in sparkling seas off Newport, RI.

Below Hang gliding in NH, another new sport.

important New England treat is tuna ("horse mackerel" the early settlers called them). So reliable is the tuna run, in fact, that tournaments are held every year in several New England ports, most notably off Block Island (RI). Tuna are exceptional swimmers (45 mph) and fierce and spectacular fighters who will test any fisherman's skill.

For the armchair sportsman, there is a rich variety of amateur and professional sports available. As well as various amateur leagues in many sports, there are 141 accredited colleges and universities in New England and most of them follow full intercollegiate schedules in the usual sports – football, hockey, basketball, baseball, track, swimming, and so on. Most of the more northerly colleges hold winter carnivals too. The Dartmouth winter carnival is the oldest and most famous. Rivalries in other sports are often among the oldest sporting fixtures in the United States (Harvard-Yale, for example). As an interesting aside it might be mentioned that the two New England teams, Harvard and Yale, each have more football All-Americans than any other universities. They have also each won more football games than any other teams in America.

Professional sports in New England means Boston – the Boston Red Sox, the Boston Bruins, the Boston Celtics, Boston Garden. Even the New England Patriots are based in a Boston suburb. For the most part being a Boston sports fan is a frustrating experience – whichever sport you follow. The Red Sox have occasionally deigned to win the World Series, The Bruins to win the Stanley Cup, but Boston teams seem to take a cantankerous New England pride in only occasionally winning the glittering prizes in their particular sports. Early leaders, middle of the tablers, runners-up, that seems to be satisfactory for a Boston team.

Of all the professional sports played in Boston, only the Celtics could truly be said to have dominated their sport. For more than a decade the Celts ruled professional basketball – New England's one sporting dynasty. Even today names like Cousy, Russell, and Auerbach are household names in New England.

The summer sport *par excellence* is sailing. The New England coast is only 473 miles long, but if all the parts of it touched by salt water – all the bays, inlets, and indentations – are tallied in, the total is closer to 6130 miles, or about a quarter of the distance around the Earth!

With its snug harbors, reliable winds, close-to-shore deep water, and spectacular scenery, the New England coast from Maine to Connecticut is perfect sailing water. (Even Vermont, the only New England state without a seacoast, offers excellent sailing on Lake Champlain and on other lakes and ponds.) It is not surprising that such a congenial coast should shelter a daunting armada of powerboats and yachts. Long Island Sound has been called "the finest sailing water in the world," but few would deny the pleasures of day cruising "down East" – the coast of Maine with its rugged shoreline and colorful harbors. Marblehead (MA) Race Week, with its harbor full of sails, testifies too to the sailing qualities of Massachusetts waters.

The most prestigious event in the New England sailing calendar is the Americas Cup held in the waters off Newport (RI) every two to four years. The United States held the Americas Cup for 133 years – the longest domination of any sport by any nation ever. This domination was rudely shattered by the Australians in the summer of 1984 with their now famous "winged keel". What sportsman would not say well done to them? A famous victory indeed! But now let's see how long it takes to get the Cup back – and who'd bet there won't be New Englanders on the crew when we do.

The woods and mountains of New England offer a full range of rock climbing and hiking. Well-run campgrounds offer facilities to suit every degree of masochism. The rivers offer white water canoeing in the spring and canoe-voyaging the rest of the year. Other sports played regularly in New England but too numerous to discuss in detail include bocce, boxing, dog sled racing, hang gliding, horse racing, jai alai, judo, karate, polo, soccer, tennis, and wrestling. Whatever your tastes, just name it. Chances are sporting New England will have it.

Left One of New England's many contributions to the 1984 Olympic triumph. Joan Benoit of Maine wins the Woman's Marathon. Step-by-step television coverage of Joan's courage and endurance moved the nation.

Right The start of the Boston Marathon, oldest and most prestigious of the many marathons that now take place in America. The race was first run in 1897.

CHAPTER 4

Yankee Ingenuity

Do you know who invented the hole in the doughnut? Do you know who invented mass production? Or the corkscrew? Or the steamboat? If you answered "a New Englander" in each case, you would be right. For three centuries New Englanders have enjoyed a reputation for ingenuity and inventiveness. A reputation well borne out by history. Where did all this creativity come from?

When the Pilgrim Fathers arrived in the New World they brought with them certain moral and intellectual qualities which were to be sharpened by their experiences in the wilderness. They were, first of all, men of firm and determined character who had overcome formidable obstacles in their lives. They were also middle-class Englishmen, often well off and educated, men who had already made their mark in the society in which they lived. But money and book learning didn't show them how to get through the winter, nor how to get their crops planted, nor their fields cleared. Being learned and articulate didn't make much impression on an Indian with a tomahawk. The wilderness asks a lot of questions, and you survived or not by your ability to find answers to these questions.

It is not surprising then that when all this Old World brainpower was turned to the daily problems of New World existence, it should be characterized by a staunch perseverance and ingenuity. The Puritans found solutions because they had to. There was nowhere else to turn. They were not merely passive receivers of the artifacts their society chose to pass on to them. They were also active makers of that society. They created not only the artifacts of the society they lived in but the very fabric of what that society would be. The individual served society and society the individual. The Puritans quickly learned that no problem was too tough if one was

Right Plymouth (MA) harbor, filled with private pleasure craft. Parts of the New England coast have been described as "the finest sailing water in the world". *Mayflower II* is moored in the foreground.

Below The oldest serving commissioned ship in any Navy in the world – the *USS Constitution* in Boston Harbor. She was nicknamed "Old Ironsides" during the War of 1812 when British cannonballs bounced off her sides.

determined enough, and this attitude was to pass on into Yankee culture.

It should be remembered too that the Puritans were radicals and dissenters. Their religious non-conformity led them to a kind of natural intellectual non-conformity. Hidebound they were in matters religious, but in practical matters they were free-wheelers. They had no hesitation in looking at problems with fresh eyes. If one solution didn't work, then try another. And if things worked well, what could be more characteristic of rugged individualists like the Puritans than to ask why they couldn't be made to work better? This cheerful intellectual non-conformity also passed into Yankee tradition. It gave New Englanders confidence in their own powers to solve the problems that faced them.

It should be remembered too that traditional creative outlets – painting, theater, dance, literature (except sermons!), and even that great English middle-class surrogate art form, gardening – did not exist in Puritan society. The creativity which might normally have been siphoned off into traditional artistic expression was turned instead to dealing with the problems of everyday existence.

Neither was there a strong university tradition – at least not in the early days. There simply weren't enough scholarships to go around – and such places as did exist were mainly for potential clerics. Knowledge in early New England was not transmitted as it is in our time through schools and universities, but by word of mouth – from father to son, mother to daughter. In the absence of expert credentials to say what it was or wasn't possible to do, ordinary men and women set out to do things for themselves. Since one

Left "The shot heard round the world." The early Revolutionary battles with which America won her independence are reconstructed yearly by public-spirited New Englanders.

Below left A Pilgrim House, Plimouth, (old spelling of Plymouth) Plantations, MA. In dwellings and clothes like these, the Pilgrims endured their first years in the wilderness.

Above The final resting place of Samuel Adams, American patriot, signer of the Declaration of Independence, Governor of Massachusetts, leading light in the Committees of Correspondence. Adams' speeches and writings inflamed the Colonists to armed revolt.

didn't understand that there were sound theoretical reasons why one *couldn't* do something, one simply went ahead and did it – a healthy skepticism which persists in New England thinking even today.

This strain of practicality and ingenuity never withered in Yankee tradition and once the basic fight for survival had been won, it was to express itself in other ways – shrewdness in business, acumen in banking, innovation in industry. The tools that settled the West – the Colt six-shooter, the Winchester rifle, and the Concord stagecoach – were all New England inventions, designed and built by New Englanders. So was the steamboat; the cotton gin; the sewing machine; steel nails; the mass-produced musket; the Springfield rifle; the M-1; lollipops on sticks; the Yankee clipper; vulcanized rubber; *and* men's sideburns. New England invented its own breeds of chicken (Rhode Island Reds and New Hampshire Reds); its own breeds of horse (Morgans and Narraganset Pacers); its own vine (the Concord Grape); its own literary/philosophical movement (Transcendentalism); even its own religion (Christian Science).

And these, of course, are just the inventions and developments that became well known. In a thousand anonymous ways Yankee ingenuity was put to the test in solving the everyday problems of the New World – *our* world. "Can do," says the Yankee and he can because he comes from a tradition which once *had* to do.

When the New England frontier was finally settled, Yankee creativity began to express itself in the more traditional ways. From the nineteenth century onward the list of writers born or bred in New England is daunting: Henry Adams, Horatio Alger, John Dewey, Emily Dickinson, Henry Wadsworth Longfellow, Robert Lowell, Sylvia Plath, Edgar Allan Poe, Harriet Beecher Stowe, Noah Webster, and John Greenleaf Whittier. Writers like Robert Frost, Stephen King, and Kenneth Roberts took up residence in New England. e.e. Cummings summered in New Hampshire, and Norman Mailer on Cape Cod. The main literary movement in New England was Transcendentalism, which flourished in and around Concord (MA) in the nineteenth century – writers like Emerson, Hawthorne, and Thoreau. In their writing there was a strong emphasis on self-reliance and individualism; one should live according to truths seen through reason. They attempted to unite manual and intellectual work. Even so it is not difficult to hear Puritan echoes in their thinking. Live simply, wrote Thoreau, and in harmony with

Facing page above A millionaire's mansion in Newport, RI. Some of the most elegant homes in America were built here during Newport's Gilded Age. Summer homes of "The 400", many of the mansions are now museums.

Facing page middle The John Hancock Inn, oldest operating inn in NH. Town and Inn were named after the signer of the Declaration of Independence who boldly wrote his name large enough so the King could read it "without using his spectacles".

Facing page bottom Beacon Hill, Boston, MA. The shutters, brickwork, and elegant proportions mark this as one of the graceful town houses of Boston's socially prominent. Many of these homes have remained in the same families for generations.

Left Old Sturbridge Village, MA. Guides in authentic nineteenth century New England dress explain the many exhibits. The graceful fan doorway is characteristic of New England architecture.

Below Shaker Village, New Gloucester, ME. Milkweed withstands the winter cold. The Shakers, an offshoot of the Quakers, are so named because their religious intensity causes them to shake during religious meetings. Shakers do not marry and are celibate. As a result, the sect is dying out.

nature. This will give you the time and energy to "live deep and suck the marrow out of life." Thoreau's essay on "Civil Disobedience" was to influence figures as diverse as Tolstoy and Gandhi.

The Puritans were to bequeath strong tradition to New England and this was their respect for education. They valued education almost as much as they did religion. From the moment of signing the Mayflower Compact aboard ship before stepping ashore for the first time, the Puritans were determined to build a just and above all democratic society (for themselves at least). They understood too that the price of democracy – and its main safeguard – was a literate, educated populace. The most powerful weapon in democracy's arsenal is a well-trained mind, free of cant, capable of arriving at its own freely and rationally made decisions. It is not surprising that the Puritans made education one of their first concerns, even at a time when their continued survival in New England was very much in doubt.

The first secondary school in the United States was founded in New England (Boston Latin, 1635); the first university (Harvard, 1636); the first elementary schools (Massachusetts, 1647); and the first free public libraries (Peterborough (NH), 1833). There are now 141 colleges and universities in New England. Four of the eight Ivy League colleges are there (Brown, Dartmouth, Harvard, Yale) as are many other famous institutions – MIT, Radcliffe, Wellesley, Smith, Brandeis, Amherst, and so on. In fact, 13 per cent of the nation's colleges and universities are in New England. So are some of the finest prep schools in the country but the state secondary systems are of such high standard that graduates can and do enter

Left Louisa May Alcott's house in Concord, MA. The author lived here while she wrote *Little Women*. Her family were prominent abolitionists, educators, temperance advocates, and feminists. Emerson, Hawthorne, Holmes, and Thoreau were family friends. Louisa May somehow also found time to serve as a nurse during the Civil War.

Below Harvard is the oldest institution of higher learning in the US, and one of the most prestigous. Six American Presidents have attended its various colleges.

directly the top academic institutions in America.

New England also has a strong musical tradition. The Boston Symphony is rated as one of the world's great orchestras and Symphony Hall is widely known for its acoustical perfection – though no one can quite explain it. The orchestra has a summer season at Tanglewood in the Berkshires where it holds concerts in the open air. The Boston Pops plays in Hatch Memorial Shell on the Charles River embankment in the summer, concerts attended by whole families sprawling on blankets on the grass. Of a lesser eminence but no less serious are a number of orchestras in other New England cities.

Professional theater is well established in Boston (though definitely *not* an inheritance from the Pilgrims), and there are serious amateur and semi-professional troupes in most population centers. Stock theater companies perform a variety of plays in the tourist season but when the summer crowds go, so do the theaters. Ballet and opera flourish in Boston. Painters as different as Andrew Wyeth and Norman Rockwell have found New England a congenial place to work in. There are artists' and writers' colonies throughout New England – some such as the MacDowell Colony (NH) were premeditated – others such as Provincetown (MA) sprang up spontaneously.

The preservation and transmission of cultural traditions is an important part of New England life. There are few towns of any size which do not have libraries or historical societies, art galleries or museums. The Puritans were undoubtedly not an easy people to get along with, but whatever their imperfections, they bequeathed a rich cultural and intellectual tradition which enriches our lives today.

Facing page above Lilies from a New Hampshire garden. The short growing season and difficult soil of New England are no problem for the skilful gardener.

Facing page Shade grown tobacco. The white cheese-cloth covering maintains a warm, even temperature to ensure optimum growing conditions. Connecticut tobacco is much sought after as wrapper for fine cigars. The farmers' main worry is hailstorms!

Below New England's very own breed of horse – the Morgan. Fast, strong, temperamentally stable and possibly the finest woods horse in the world, the Morgan was developed in Vermont in the eighteenth century.

Left The Great North Woods. Hemlock boughs on a rainy day.

Below The Rhode Island Red (pictured here) and the New Hampshire Red are two breeds of chicken developed in New England. They are valued world wide for their outstanding egg-laying and meat-bearing qualities.

Right Norman Rockwell, well-loved painter of Americana with his Boy Scout Calendars and *Saturday Evening Post* covers, lived in Arlington, VT. Here, George Zimmer, one of Rockwell's many local models, proudly displays a cover painting of him Rockwell did for the *Post*. Many of Rockwell's *Post* covers depicted scenes in and around Arlington.

Below The Northeast Old Time Fiddlers Association holds annual banjo and fiddling contests. New Englanders value such musical events just as much as they do performances by their leading orchestra – the Boston Symphony – one of the finest orchestras in the world.

Left Ella Fitzgerald, one of the many world-famous stars who has appeared at the Newport Jazz Festival.

Below A contestant gives his all at the Old Time Fiddlers' Contest held in Newfane, VT.

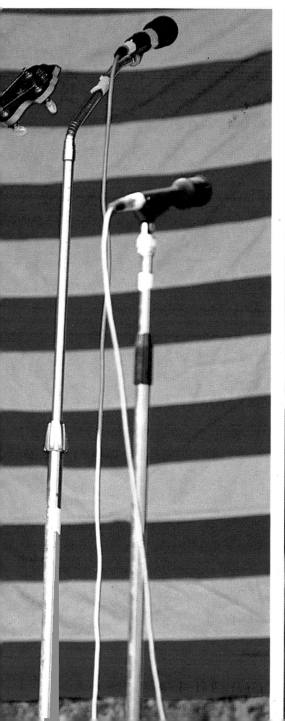

CHAPTER 5

Spirit of New England

Geographically, New England consists of six small states huddled together in the northeast corner of America. So small are they, that even added together they cover an area smaller than the state of Washington. New England is shaped roughly like a triangle with New York to the west, Canada to the north, and the long ragged coastline with the Atlantic Ocean forming the east-to-south hypotenuse.

Northern New England (Maine, New Hampshire, Vermont) tends on the whole to be rural, Republican, agricultural, and conservative (in speech and manners as well as in politics). Southern New England (Massachusetts, Rhode Island, Connecticut), as it is slowly sucked into the vast East Coast conurbation that sprawls between Washington and New York, tends increasingly to be urban, Democratic, industrialized, and relatively liberal (always a comparative term in New England).

Despite differences, however, the New England states are remarkably similar in outlook and character; certainly they resemble each other more than they resemble other parts of America. The region is so small and compact that very little – from Revolution to Recession – happens to one state that does not happen to them all. The long western border with New York cuts New England off from the rest of the United States (a fact which the British Army tried – unsuccessfully – to exploit in the Revolution). Perhaps it is this that gives New England its sense of unity and autonomy – its feel of a region apart.

It has often been said that New England is the one part of the United States which could drift away from the rest and still exist as a viable entity, complete and self-sufficient in itself; quite possibly this is true – even in today's interdependent world. It is certainly an idea which would appeal to many New Englanders. "Yankee cussedness" is as much in evidence as it ever was, particularly in the smaller towns.

Small towns have remained the least changed part of New England. There is new building in the outskirts but the central parts of the towns remain untouched. There is still the square and the church, picket fences, quiet tree-lined streets, the public park with its traditional flagpole, the post office, the well-tended graveyard. Nor has the independent spirit of the people changed much either as anyone who has ever attended a New England Town Meeting can testify.

The Town Meeting is a particularly New England institution. It is quite literally a meeting of everyone who lives in a particular town. At these meetings, the townsfolk will vote directly on the issues that affect their lives – whether to paint the town hall, whether or not to raise property taxes, and so on. Anyone who lives there may discuss any issue in as much depth as he wishes. No holds are barred. In the most direct way possible government is held to account by the governed. Tempers can run high. It is possibly the purest form of democracy there is. Most towns have no objections to visitors attending their meetings and anyone who wants to see democracy in action could do worse than to start here.

So autonomous are New England towns that they are called "little republics". They have "home rule" which means that on most issues even their own state legislatures cannot overrule them.

A few stories might help illustrate the spirit of New England towns. In 1684, King Charles II revoked the Royal Charter of Massachusetts Bay Colony. This so incensed the inhabitants of the town of Quinsigamond (MA) that they promptly changed the name of their town to Worcester. Worcester, you may remember, was the town where Charles's army suffered a heavy defeat at the hands of the Roundheads. Or take 1776. When the town of Litchfield (CN) heard news of the Revolution, they promptly melted down a lead statue of George III and turned it into 42 000 musket balls for the Colonial Army. Or in more modern times take the case of a lady who moved to a small New England town. For ten years she tried to make friends with the local ladies but to no avail. Everyone seemed to avoid her. This was a longish time to avoid getting acquainted even by New England standards. Eventually the lady found out why. It seems that when she put out her laundry to dry, she didn't hang her underwear inside the pillow cases!

Right Atop Mt Chicorua overlooking the rain squalls in the distance.

Left Provincetown, MA, on the tip of Cape Cod, is swollen each year by the arrival of a vast summer population which far outnumbers the locals. P-town, as it is known to New Englanders, has a thriving artist's colony. A German submarine bombarded nearby sand dunes during WWI.

Below This famous old lobster shack at Rockport, MA, has been painted so often that it came to be known as "American Motif Number One." Heavily damaged in the blizzards of 1978, the shack was rebuilt by popular demand.

New England cities have undergone severe changes in recent times. In the 1920s and 1930s, the textile industry sought lower transport and labor costs by moving south. Overnight, cities like Manchester (NH) were on the verge of bankruptcy, a condition further intensified by the Great Depression. The cities fought back by diversifying and luring new industries to the area. In Manchester, what had once been the largest cotton mill in the world became instead a conglomerate of diversified industries, manufacturing everything from exposure meters to potato chips. In more recent times, most New England cities have had to face the usual urban problems. Loss of their tax base to the suburbs, sub-standard housing, decaying downtown areas fighting for business with suburban shopping centers, urban sprawl. Once again the cities have fought back courageously and imaginatively with new building – malls and shopping centers, office complexes and housing developments – right in the heart of town; ingenious attacks on traffic and parking problems; and stricter zoning laws. Constitution Plaza and the tall new buildings added to the skyline of Hartford (CN) are typical of the urban renewal projects with which New England cities prepare for the twenty-first century.

Even Boston, the largest New England city, is not exempt from such problems. If anything, its urban problems are worse. They started earlier, their effects are more widespread and are exacerbated by racial tensions. Half the people who live in New England live in Massachusetts; half the peole who live in Massachusetts live in Greater Boston.

With a combination of Federal and State money, however, Boston has rebuilt on a large scale – preserving historic landmarks such as Fanueil Hall, but sweeping away buildings which had served their useful life span and replacing them with a bustling new downtown. Private money, too, has built high-rise complexes like the Prudential and John Hancock Towers.

Facing page The Fourth of July parade, Jamaica, VT. Almost every town in New England celebrates the Fourth. Youngsters decorate their bicycles with red, white, and blue bunting. There are speeches, parades, bands, fairs and fireworks.

Left New England bequeathed Thanksgiving to the nation. The first Thanksgiving celebrated in 1621, also included clams, oysters, deer, geese, ducks, fish, succotash and johnnycake. In fact it was the Indians, not the Pilgrims who brought turkeys to the feast.

Below Montville Town Meeting, ME. Here the citizens and selectmen of a town discuss and vote on the issues that affect their lives. New England Town Meetings are possibly the purest form of democracy there is.

Bottom Children "helping out" at the watermelon stall of a Fourth of July fair. A childhood in rural New England is usually recalled fondly by those fortunate enough to have experienced one. Jamaica, VT.

Despite urban renewal, the charm of historic Old Boston remains intact – as well it should. Many of the events that sparked off the American Revolution took place in and around Boston and many of the most ardent patriots lived there, so much so that Boston has been called "the Cradle of Liberty." The best way to see historic Boston is by following the Freedom Trail, a marked path one and a half miles long which takes one past many of the historic sites of the Revolution – Fanueil Hall where angry Colonists protested against the hated stamp and tea taxes; the Old South Meeting House, where certain "Indians" met before a certain tea party; the Old North Church, where Paul Revere saw his famous lanterns ("One if by land, two if by sea, and I on the opposite shore will be ..."). One can also visit the Bunker Hill Battle site ("Don't fire till you see the whites of their eyes!"), and it is well worth crossing the Harbor to visit *Old Ironsides* (British cannonballs used to bounce off her), the oldest serving ship in any navy in the world. Lexington and Concord, where the fighting actually began, are only a short ride out of town.

Boston is a city of many fine museums and galleries, and Boston Common, with its swanboats, has a surprising charm. So does Beacon Hill with its crooked streets and gracious eighteenth-century buildings. The market in the North End is well worth a visit. Downtown has many fine stores and restaurants and seafood is a local specialty.

One of Boston's most famous regional dishes (apart from beans) is called "scrod", a dish made from tender young codfish. A gourmet from the Midwest is alleged to have jumped into a cab in Boston and asked, "Hey, where can I get scrod?" The driver turned to him and said, "Buddy, guys've been asking me that question for twenty years, but you're the first one I ever heard ask for it in the past pluperfect subjunctive!"

Boston is not the town it was three and a half centuries ago. It has changed vastly. And so has the rest of New England. A complex new society has grown up, new cultures have been absorbed, the ideals of the Pilgrim Fathers have been re-examined and fitted to the needs of our own time. In an eyeblink of history, New England has changed from wilderness to farming, from farming to manufacturing, from manufacturing to industry. Yes, New England has changed – but, then again, it hasn't.

Facing page Harvest time in New England. Newtown, CT.

Left Reshingling a New England house. Wood, cheap and abundant, has traditionally been an important source of building material in heavily-forested New England. Even the Indians made wigwams out of bark and reed mats laid out as shingles on top of saplings.

Below One of the many antique shops that flourish in New England. Be careful with the china because most Yankee shops have the same rule; if you drop it, you've bought it!

Facing page The tear-drop shape of the Phoenix Life Headquarters in Hartford, CT, typifies the dynamic new skyline of America's "Insurance Capital." As in many New England cities, decaying downtowns have been replaced by vital and exciting new constructions.

Right Ship building has always been a thriving industry on the New England coast, for both private and naval vessels. Here, a Trident submarine is being constructed by General Dynamics of Groton, CT. Across the Thames river, in New London, is the HQ of the North Atlantic Fleet

Below Unloading potatoes in Searsport, ME. Maine is the leading potato growing state east of the Mississippi.

Facing page The John Hancock Building, Boston. Glimpses of Trinity Church are reflected in the gleaming sides of this magnificent building, tallest skyscraper in New England.

Right Open air checkers, chess and dominoes in the courtyard of the Old North Church are part of Boston tradition.

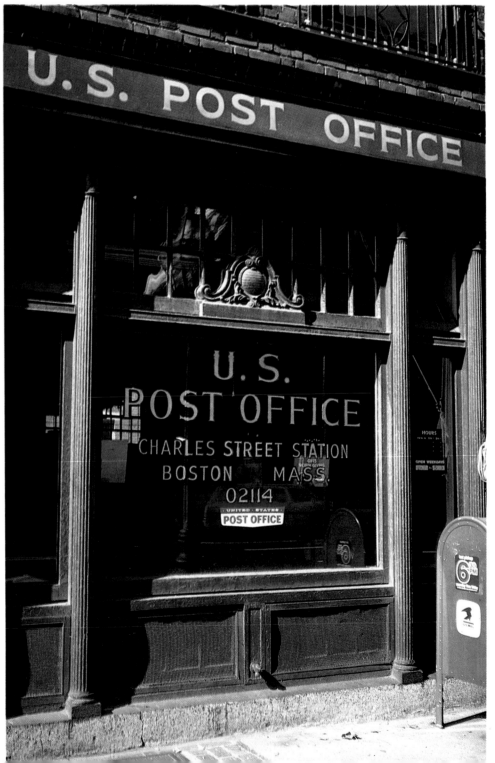

Above The golden dome of the New State House, Boston, MA. once said to be the "hub around which the universe revolved". The New State House was designed by Charles Bulfinch who then went on to design the National Capitol in Washington.

Right Many areas of Boston retain their village flavor. Charles Street Post Office, at the foot of Beacon Hill, could be a rural Post Office in any small town in New England.

Observatory and
Visitor Information

Facing page Typical of the way old blends with new in Boston, Park Street Church stands in the middle of the downtown shopping area. Government troops stored gunpowder here in the War of 1812. In 1829, William Lloyd Garrison made the first of his abolitionist speeches from its pulpit.

Left Christian Science was founded in New England by Mary Baker Eddy of New Hampshire. Here we see the quiet elegance of the interior of the Mother Church in Boston – world headquarters of Christian Science.

Below Fanueil Hall, Boston, with its famous grasshopper weathervane. Angry Colonists met here to protest British injustices in the years leading up to the Revolution. During the War of 1812, strangers who could not identify the grasshopper as the symbol of Boston were questioned as spies.

Below Boston's North End is now the home of a large Italian population. There are Italian shops and restaurants and Italian is heard spoken in the streets.

Facing page Boston Public Gardens, the oldest botanical park in America, lies side by side with Boston Common, the oldest public park. The pedal-powered swan boats are part of the Garden's enduring charm, but watch out for the pigeons flying overhead.

Right Quincy Market, in the North End of Boston. During the summer, the mostly Italian population of this part of Boston celebrates Saint's days with parades and colorful fiestas.

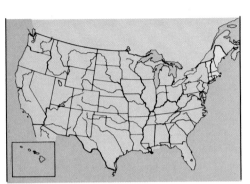

NEW ENGLAND

MAINE

Bangor

⑪ STOWE
BURLINGTON

⑩ ACADIA NAT. PK.
FRENCHMAN BAY
ISLE AU HAUTE

VERMONT

WHITE MOUNTAINS

GREEN MOUNTAINS

⑫ LACONIA

PORTLAND

NEW HAMPSHIRE
CONCORD

PORTSMOUTH

Manchester

MASSACHUSETTS

BERKSHIRE HILLS

② LEXINGTON
③ CAMBRIDGE
Boston

⑮

⑤ CAPE COD

• Springfield

④ STURBRIDGE

PLYMOUTH
①

⑭ HARTFORD

CONNECTICUT

PAWTUCKET
⑧ Providence
RHODE ISLAND

⑨
NEWPORT
⑦

NEW BEDFORD

Newhaven

MARTHAS VINEYARD

NANTUCKET ISLAND

Bridgeport

The Minuteman Statue

1 See the **Mayflower II,** an exact replica of the tiny ship that carried the Pilgrims to the New World. It is moored at Plimouth Plantations, MA. Plimouth is a reconstruction of the colonists' first home in the New World, built as it looked in the year 1627.

2 The **Minuteman Statue,** at Lexington, MA. The opening battle of the American Revolution was fought by these volunteer soldiers, who, at all times were fit and trained, capable of fighting "at a minute's notice".

3 **Harvard University** at Cambridge, MA. Founded in 1636, Harvard is the oldest institution of higher learning in the US.

4 **Sturbridge Village,** MA is an accurate reconstruction of a New England town in the early nineteenth century.

5 **Cape Cod.** The population is swollen each year by the arrival of a vast summer influx. Provincetown, on the tip of Cape Cod, has a thriving artist's colony.

6 **Autumn.** Visitors come from all over the world to see New England in the fall. At the height of the New England fall it is like being transported to another planet, the colors are so spectacular.

7 The **Americas Cup,** held every two to four years off Newport, RI, is the most important event in the yachting calendar.

8 The **State Capital,** Providence RI has the second largest unsupported marble dome in the world after St Peter's in Rome.

Fanueil Hall

Harvard University

Acadia National Park

The Newport Jazz Festival

The State Capital

9 The **Newport Jazz Festival** attracts many internationally-known jazz stars.

10 **Acadia National Park,** Maine contains the most dramatic scenery along the coast. It is a perfect combination of surf, rock and forest.

11 **Stowe,** Vt. Skiing is particularly popular in the winter.

12 **Laconia,** NH is the scene of the world dog sled championships.

13 The **Boston Marathon** is the oldest and most prestigious of the many marathons run in America. It was first run in 1897.

14 **Mark Twain's House,** Hartford, CN. The author lived and wrote in this house for 20 years.

15 **Fanueil Hall,** Boston was the meeting place for angry Colonists protesting against British injustices.

Autumn

PICTURE CREDITS